Dragonfly Where Change Takes Flight

TRANSFORMING ADVERSITY INTO STRENGTH TO SOAR BEYOND SETBACKS

Tammy Corwin

Words Matter Publishing
P.O. Box 1190
Decatur, Il 62525
www.wordsmatterpublishing.com

ISBN 13: 978-1-962467-33-9

Library of Congress Catalog Card Number: 2024942613

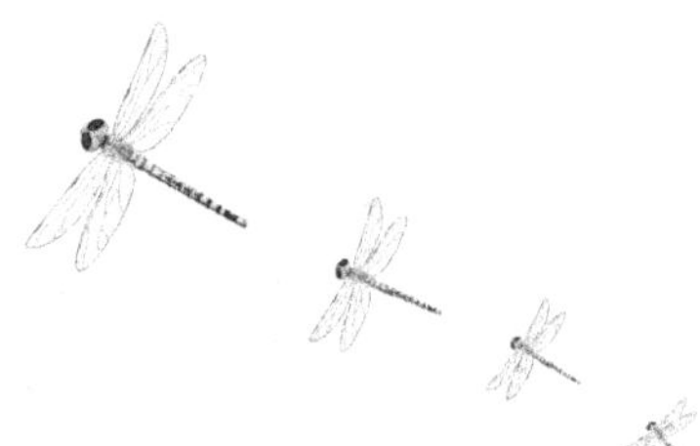

Preface:
Understanding the Dragonfly Concept

Dragonflies are fascinating creatures that embody a blend of natural wonder, ecological importance, and cultural symbolism. Here is a detailed account covering their life cycle, unique abilities, and spiritual meanings:

1. Metamorphosis of a Dragonfly

Dragonflies undergo a remarkable transformation in their life cycle, which consists of three stages: egg, nymph, and adult.

- **Egg:** The life of a dragonfly starts when a female lays her eggs on or near water. Depending on the species, eggs can be inserted into aquatic plants or simply dropped into the water.

- **Nymph (Larva):** Dragonfly eggs hatch into nymphs, which live underwater for a significant part of their life cycle, which can last anywhere from a few months to several years, depending on the species and environmental conditions. Dragonfly nymphs are voracious predators, feeding on other aquatic larvae, tadpoles, and even small fish. They undergo numerous molts as they grow, shedding their exoskeleton several times.

- **Adult:** The final stage of their transformation, known as emergence, occurs when the nymph feels ready to transition into adulthood. It climbs up a reed or other suitable substrate and emerges from its final nymphal skin. The new adult, known as a teneral, is soft-bodied initially and highly vulnerable until its exoskeleton hardens and wings fully develop. Adult dragonflies live for a few weeks to several months, during which they mate, and the females lay eggs to begin the cycle anew.

2. Skills of a Dragonfly

Dragonflies are adept flyers, capable of incredible feats that make them formidable hunters.

- **Flight:** Dragonflies can fly straight up and down, hover like a helicopter, and even mate mid-air. They can reach speeds up to 30 miles per hour and can suddenly change their flight direction.

- **Vision:** One of the most distinctive features of dragonflies is their large, multifaceted eyes, which provide nearly 360-degree vision. This exceptional sight allows them to perceive movements and track prey with astounding accuracy.

3. Spiritual Meaning of a Dragonfly

In many cultures, dragonflies symbolize change, adaptability, and self-realization. Their ability to move in all six directions and their habit of being near water often symbolize the unconscious or deeper thoughts surfacing.

- **Change and Adaptability:** The dragonfly's life cycle, from nymph to adult, symbolizes transformation and the ability to adapt to new environments, mirroring personal growth.

- **Illusion:** In some Native American beliefs, dragonflies are seen as shape-shifters or illusionists, reminding us that things are not always as they appear.

4. Additional Facts and Significance

- **Ecological Role:** As both predators and prey, dragonflies play a vital role in the aquatic and terrestrial food chains. They help control populations of harmful insects like mosquitoes and flies.

- **Indicator Species:** Dragonflies are also considered indicators of ecological health. The diversity and population of dragonflies in an area can help gauge the health of an ecosystem, particularly aquatic environments.

Conclusion

Dragonflies not only capture our imagination with their beauty and flight skills but also contribute significantly to ecological balance and reflect deep cultural meanings. Their presence is a reminder of the importance of adaptability, the illusion of perception, and the ever-present possibility of transformation in our lives.

Outline and Table of Contents

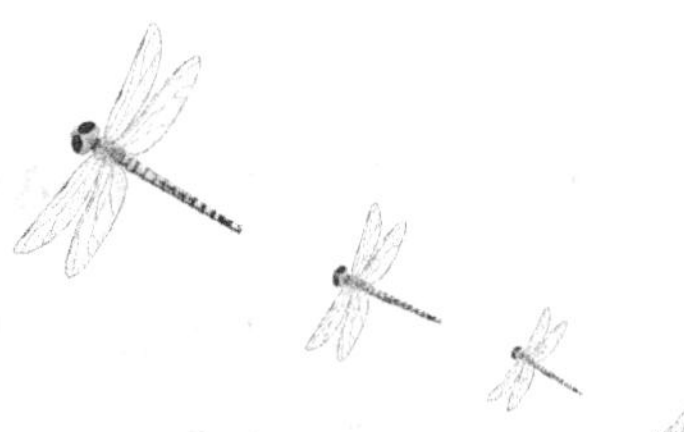

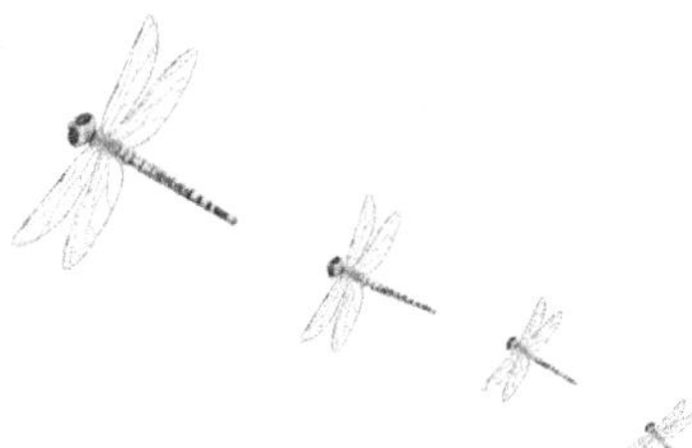

Becoming a Dragonfly: An Introduction

In the journey of life, few symbols capture the essence of transformation as profoundly as the dragonfly. From its humble beginnings as a nymph in the water to its eventual ascent into the air with iridescent wings, the dragonfly embodies resilience, adaptability, and a profound metamorphosis. This book, "Dragonfly Where Change Takes Flight," is your guide through a similar transformation of the self—aimed at those who have faced loss, endured trauma, and are seeking not just to recover but to redefine their existence.

Throughout the following chapters, you will be guided through ten transformative steps, each serving as a milestone on your journey to a new beginning. These steps are designed to help you understand where you stand, set and achieve your goals, cultivate resilience, practice forgiveness, overcome trauma, manage grief, and ultimately, reinvent yourself.

As you turn each page, remember that every step forward, no matter how small, is a part of your transformation. Like the dragonfly, you are evolving into something new, vibrant, and powerful. Let this book be a companion in your journey, offering insights and actions that light your path forward.

Now, let us begin at the beginning, which is understanding and accepting where you are right now.

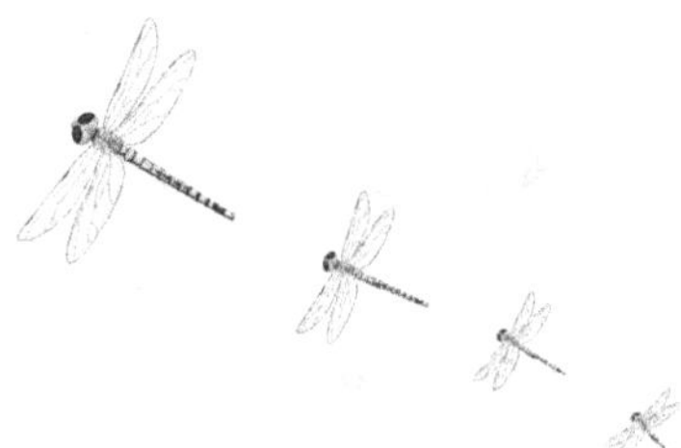

Chapter 1

Understanding Your Current State

Recognizing and Accepting Your Feelings

Step one on your journey to transformation is to fully understand your current state. This involves an honest assessment of your emotions and the circumstances that have shaped them. It is a crucial foundation, because acknowledging where you are is the first step in deciding where you wish to go.

Self-Assessment

Begin with a self-assessment. This process can be challenging, as it requires confronting potentially painful emotions and admitting truths you might have avoided. Start by asking yourself a series of questions:

1. What are the predominant emotions I feel daily?

2. What triggers these emotions?

3. How do these emotions affect my thoughts and behaviors?

Documenting your answers will be helpful. Writing not only helps in organizing thoughts but also in recognizing patterns that emerge over time.

Acceptance

Acceptance is acknowledging the reality of your situation without judgment. It does not mean resignation or giving up. Rather, it's an acknowledgment of your current realities, which lays the groundwork for change. Techniques to facilitate acceptance include mindfulness meditation and cognitive reframing. Here's a simple exercise to begin practicing acceptance:

- **Mindfulness Meditation:** Spend five minutes each day in a quiet space, focusing solely on your breathing. As thoughts about your circumstances arise, acknowledge them without judgment and gently bring your focus back to your breath.

- **Cognitive Reframing:** Change the narrative of your thoughts from negative to neutral or positive. For instance, instead of thinking, "I can't get past this," reframe it to, "I am facing challenges, but I am working on overcoming them."

As you work through these exercises, remember that understanding and accepting your current state doesn't happen overnight. It is the first essential step on your path to profound transformation.

Notes

Chapter 2

Embracing Change

Welcoming the Winds of Change

Change is the only constant in life, yet it is often feared and resisted. Embracing change is crucial to transformation, just as a dragonfly must surrender to its nature to metamorphose. In this chapter, we will explore the nature of change, understand why it can be so daunting, and learn practical ways to embrace it, making peace with the unknown and turning uncertainty into action.

Understanding Change

Change involves moving from the known to the unknown, which can provoke anxiety and uncertainty. It often involves a shift in our environment, routines, relationships, or ourselves. Recognizing that change is a necessary part of growth helps in adapting and thriving.

1. The Psychology of Change

- Change can trigger a loss of control, fear of the unknown, and discomfort with new situations. Understanding these feelings can help you manage your reactions to change.

- **Reflective Exercise:** Write down a list of changes you've experienced in the past year. Note your initial reactions to these changes and how you feel about them now. This can help you see how you've adapted over time, even to unexpected shifts.

2. The Cycle of Change

- **Change often follows a cycle:** a period of ending, followed by a neutral zone, and then a new beginning. Recognizing which part of the cycle you are in can help you navigate through it more effectively.

- **Visual Mapping:** Create a visual map of a recent major change in your life, identifying these three stages. This exercise helps in understanding and accepting each phase's impact and duration.

Embracing Uncertainty

The uncertainty that comes with change can be paralyzing, but embracing it is a powerful step towards personal growth and resilience.

1. Strategies for Embracing Uncertainty

- **Stay Present:** Focus on the current moment rather than worrying about what the future holds. Techniques such as mindfulness and meditation can aid in this.

- **Build Flexibility:** Developing a flexible mindset allows you to better adapt to changing circumstances. Practice thinking of multiple outcomes to situations to enhance your adaptability.

2. Making Peace with the Unknown

- **Cultivate Curiosity:** Instead of fearing the unknown, try to view changes as opportunities to learn and grow. Adopt a curious mindset about what lies ahead.

- **Reframe Your Perspective:** Shift your view of uncertainty from a threat to an adventure. This reframing can transform your emotional and behavioral responses to change.

Turning Uncertainty into Action

Action alleviates anxiety. By taking proactive steps, you can shape how change affects you, rather than being passively shaped by it.

1. Small Steps Forward

- Breakdown overwhelming changes into manageable actions. Setting small, achievable goals can help you move forward without feeling overwhelmed.

- **Actionable Tip:** Each morning, set a small goal that aligns with the new changes you're adapting to. Completing it will give you a sense of control and progress.

2. Seek Support

- Change can feel isolating, but you don't have to go through it alone. Seeking support from friends, family, or support groups can provide comfort and advice.

- **Community Engagement:** Join a group or workshop where people are dealing with similar changes. Sharing experiences and coping strategies can be incredibly supportive.

Conclusion

Embracing change is not about eliminating fear but about learning to move forward despite it. Like the dragonfly, which must let go of its former self to emerge with new wings, you too can learn to navigate through the winds of change with grace and strength. By understanding, embracing, and acting upon the changes in your life, you prepare the ground for the profound transformation that "Becoming a Dragonfly" promises.

In the next chapter, we will explore how to set concrete and achievable goals that align with your new path, providing clear direction as you continue your journey of transformation.

Notes

Chapter 3

Setting Concrete Goals
Charting a Path Forward

Goal-setting is not just about deciding where you want to go; it's about breaking down the journey into attainable steps. In this chapter, we explore how to set effective and realistic goals that resonate with your personal aspirations and the transformation you seek. By defining clear objectives, you can maintain focus, measure progress, and stay motivated, even when challenges arise.

Understanding Goal-Setting

Effective goals provide direction and a benchmark for determining progress. They transform visions into actionable steps and are essential for any significant change or personal growth initiative.

1. The Importance of S.M.A.R.T Goals

- **Specific:** Clearly define what you want to achieve. Ambiguity can lead to inaction.

- **Measurable:** Establish concrete criteria for measuring progress toward the attainment of each goal.

- **Achievable:** Ensure that the goals are attainable; unrealistic goals can demotivate you.

- **Relevant:** Goals should be relevant to the direction you want your life to take.

- **Time-bound:** Set a deadline for completion to create urgency and prompt action.

2. The Role of Goals in Transformation

- Goals act as stepping stones in your journey of transformation, each one a milestone that marks progress and builds confidence.

Setting Your Goals

The process of setting goals should be thoughtful and deliberate. It begins with self-reflection and understanding what is genuinely important to you.

1. Reflect on Your Values and Desires

- Spend time considering what matters most to you. What aspects of your life do you want to change or improve?

- **Reflective Exercise:** Create a vision board or write a vision statement that represents your ideal future. This visual or descriptive representation can clarify your aspirations.

2. Define Your Long-term and Short-term Goals

- **Long-term Goals:** These are your major objectives, which may take several years to achieve. They represent your larger vision.

- **Short-term Goals:** These are smaller, more immediate goals that serve as steps towards achieving your long-term goals. They should be actionable within a shorter timeframe, like a year or less.

3. Prioritize Your Goals

- With all potential goals laid out, decide which are most urgent and important. Prioritizing helps you avoid feeling overwhelmed and ensures you allocate your time and resources effectively.

- **Prioritization Technique:** Use tools like the Eisenhower Box (urgent vs. important matrix) to categorize and prioritize goals based on their importance and urgency.

Creating an Action Plan

Every goal needs a clear action plan that outlines how you will achieve it. This plan includes specific actions, resources needed, potential barriers, and strategies to overcome them.

1. Break Goals into Manageable Tasks

- Divide each goal into smaller, specific tasks. This makes the goal less daunting and provides clear next steps.

- **Action Item Example:** If your goal is to improve your physical health, one task might be to schedule and plan meals weekly.

2. Set Deadlines and Milestones

- Assign deadlines to each task and establish milestones that will help you track progress.

- **Regular Review:** Set regular intervals, such as weekly or monthly, to review your progress. Adjust plans as necessary to stay on track.

3. Accountability

- Share your goals with a trusted friend, family member, or mentor who can help keep you accountable.

- **Accountability Check-in:** Arrange regular meetings or check-ins to report on your progress. This can motivate you to keep moving forward.

Conclusion

Setting concrete goals transforms abstract aspirations into tangible targets. As you progress from one goal to the next, you not only come closer to realizing your vision but also build a foundation of skills and confidence that support all areas of your life. Just as the dragonfly emerges stronger and more capable, so too will you grow through the pursuit and achievement of your goals.

In the next chapter, we will delve into cultivating resilience, a critical skill that supports you in persisting toward your goals, especially when faced with challenges.

Notes

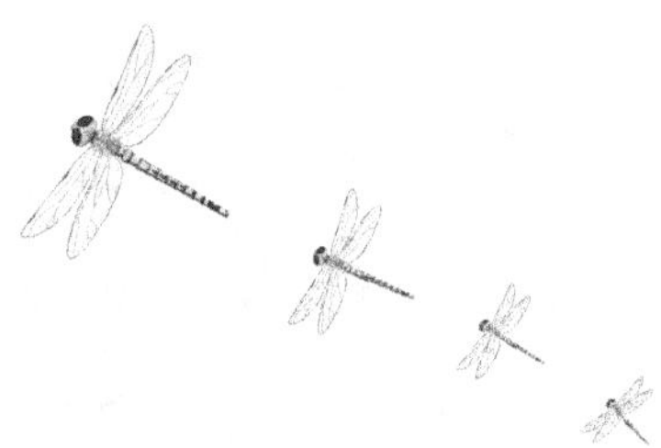

Chapter 4

Cultivating Resilience

Strengthening Your Inner Foundation

Resilience is the ability to bounce back from setbacks and challenges. It's a crucial quality in the journey of transformation, as it allows you to navigate through difficulties with strength and grace. This chapter focuses on building resilience, offering practical strategies to enhance your ability to withstand and grow from life's inevitable stresses and adversities.

Understanding Resilience

Resilience is not a trait that people either have or do not have. It involves behaviors, thoughts, and actions that can be learned and developed by anyone. A resilient person is not only able to handle difficulties but can emerge stronger from them.

1. Components of Resilience

- **Emotional Awareness:** Understanding and managing your emotions effectively.

- **Perseverance:** Persisting in the face of setbacks.

- **Optimism:** Maintaining a hopeful outlook on life.

- **Flexibility:** Adapting to new conditions and challenges.

- **Support Networks:** Building and relying on relationships for support.

2. The Role of Resilience in Transformation

- Resilience is key to not just surviving but thriving through change. It allows you to take setbacks as learning opportunities and not as defeats.

Building Mental and Emotional Resilience

Developing resilience is a personal journey that involves strengthening your mental and emotional skills.

1. Enhance Emotional Intelligence

- **Self-awareness:** Regularly practice mindfulness to better understand your emotions and triggers.

- **Self-regulation:** Develop strategies to calm your mind and body when stressed, such as deep breathing, meditation, or physical exercise.

2. Practice Perseverance

- Perseverance can be fostered by setting clear goals and maintaining a commitment to achieve them, regardless of obstacles.

- **Persistence Exercise:** When faced with a challenge, instead of giving up, ask yourself, "What is one thing I can do right now to make progress?" This approach can help maintain momentum.

3. Cultivate Optimism

- Optimism isn't about ignoring the negative, but rather about maintaining a perspective that the future holds positive possibilities.

- **Optimism Practice:** Start a gratitude journal where you record things you are thankful for daily. This can shift focus from what's going wrong to what's going right.

Strategies for Enduring Hardship

Learning to effectively manage hardships is essential for building resilience.

1. Develop Problem-Solving Skills

- Work on becoming a better problem solver by practicing systematic approaches to challenges, such as breaking them down into smaller, more manageable parts.

- **Problem-Solving Technique:** Use the "Five Whys" method to get to the root cause of a problem by asking "why" five times.

2. Build a Support System

- Strong relationships are foundational to resilience. They provide emotional support, practical help, and a sense of belonging.

- **Support-Building Tip:** Regularly connect with friends and family, join groups with similar interests, or seek professional help if needed.

3. Accept and Adapt to Change

- Acceptance does not mean resignation but recognizing the reality of the situation without struggle.

- **Flexibility Exercise:** Regularly put yourself in new situations that require you to adapt. This could be as simple as changing your routine or trying a new hobby.

Conclusion

Resilience is a dynamic combination of thoughts, behaviors, and actions that can be nurtured and developed over time. By understanding and practicing the components of resilience, you prepare yourself to face life's challenges with confidence and emerge from them stronger and more capable. This foundational strength supports every step of your transformation journey, enabling you to move closer to your goals with determination and hope.

In the next chapter, we will explore the essential practice of forgiveness, which plays a pivotal role in healing and moving forward in life.

Notes

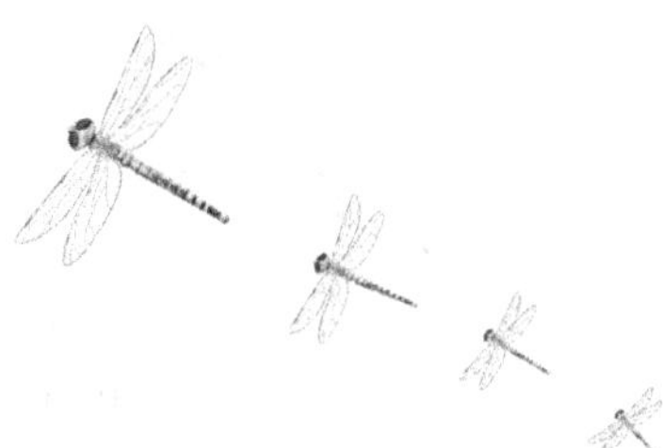

Chapter 5

Practicing Forgiveness

Healing Through Letting Go

Forgiveness is a powerful step in the journey of transformation. It involves letting go of grievances and resentments, which can free up emotional energy that is better spent on positive growth. This chapter delves into the practice of forgiveness towards oneself and others, exploring its benefits and providing practical steps to cultivate a forgiving mindset.

Understanding Forgiveness

Forgiveness is not about condoning wrongdoings or forgetting the pain caused. Instead, it is about releasing the burden of anger and resentment to make way for peace and personal growth.

1. Benefits of Forgiveness

- **Emotional Relief:** Holding onto anger ties you to the past. Forgiveness can relieve this emotional burden, improving mental health.

- **Improved Relationships:** Forgiveness can mend and strengthen relationships, creating healthier social interactions.
- **Increased Wellbeing:** Letting go of grudges reduces stress, lowering the risk of chronic health problems like heart disease.

2. The Challenges of Forgiveness

- Forgiving can be one of the hardest processes, especially when deep hurt is involved. It requires strength to look beyond the pain and see the potential for healing.

Forgiving Oneself

Self-forgiveness is crucial for self-acceptance and moving forward. It allows you to acknowledge mistakes without being defined by them.

1. Recognize Your Human Nature

- Acknowledge that making mistakes is a part of being human. Reflect on the intent behind your actions and what you have learned from them.
- **Reflection Exercise:** Write a letter to yourself describing the mistake, what it taught you, and why you deserve forgiveness.

2. Address Regrets and Guilt

- Understand the difference between healthy remorse, which leads to learning, and destructive guilt, which can paralyze.
- **Guilt Management Strategy:** Convert guilt into action by making amends where possible and committing to better choices in the future.

Forgiving Others

Forgiving others can be even more challenging than forgiving oneself, but it is equally vital for emotional liberation and relationship healing.

1. Empathy and Understanding

- Try to see the situation from the other person's perspective. This does not justify their actions but can help you understand their motives and vulnerabilities.
- **Empathy Exercise:** Imagine the other person's background, pressures, and struggles that may have influenced their actions.

2. Letting Go of the Need for Revenge

- Releasing the desire for revenge or retribution is essential in true forgiveness. This shift focuses on recovery and growth rather than punishment.
- **Letting Go Practice:** Whenever thoughts of revenge surface, redirect your energy toward something that brings you peace or joy.

Practical Steps to Cultivate Forgiveness

Developing a forgiving mindset takes time and effort. Here are some practical steps to encourage this transformational practice:

1. Practice Regular Reflection

- Reflect on incidents that cause resentment and consciously decide to work on forgiveness.
- **Daily Reflection:** End each day by noting any feelings of bitterness and making a commitment to process and release them.

2. Use Affirmations and Meditation

- Affirmations can reinforce your commitment to forgiveness, while meditation can provide the mental space needed to process emotions.

- **Forgiveness Meditation:** Focus on breathing and, with each exhale, envision letting go of anger and resentment.

Conclusion

Forgiveness is a complex yet vital part of transforming your life. It requires courage, empathy, and understanding. By learning to forgive, you not only heal your past wounds but also pave the way for future happiness and inner peace. As you master the art of forgiveness, you'll find yourself more capable of facing life's challenges with a clear and compassionate heart.

In the next chapter, we will address overcoming trauma, an essential aspect of healing and moving forward from painful experiences.

Notes

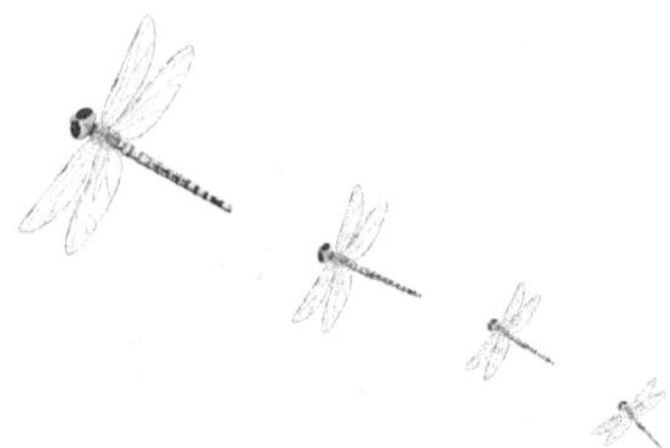

Chapter 6

Overcoming Trauma
Rebuilding After Painful Experiences

Trauma can profoundly impact life, altering one's sense of safety and self. Overcoming trauma is crucial for personal transformation, as it enables individuals to reclaim their lives and discover strength and resilience. This chapter focuses on understanding trauma, its effects, and practical strategies for healing and overcoming these deep-seated wounds.

Understanding Trauma

Trauma results from extremely stressful events that shatter your sense of security, leading to feelings of helplessness and vulnerability. It can stem from a single event or a series of events that compound over time.

1. Types of Trauma

- **Acute Trauma:** Results from a single, distressing event, such as an accident or natural disaster.

- **Chronic Trauma:** Repeated and prolonged exposure to highly stressful situations, like domestic violence or long-term illness.

- **Complex Trauma:** Exposure to varied and multiple traumatic events, often invasive and interpersonal in nature.

2. Effects of Trauma

- Emotional and psychological symptoms include shock, denial, confusion, anger, anxiety, and depression.

- Physical symptoms may involve insomnia, fatigue, being easily startled, and changes in appetite.

Techniques for Healing Trauma

Healing from trauma is possible, though it often requires time, patience, and support. Below are methods to aid in the recovery process.

1. Professional Therapy

- Seeking help from a mental health professional can be crucial. Therapies like Cognitive Behavioral Therapy (CBT), Eye Movement Desensitization and Reprocessing (EMDR), and trauma-focused therapy are highly effective.

- **Finding a Therapist:** Look for a licensed professional skilled in trauma recovery. Support groups can also offer a community of understanding and shared experiences.

2. Building a Safe Environment

- Creating a safe physical and emotional environment is foundational in trauma recovery.

- **Safety Strategies:** Establish routines that provide stability. Surround yourself with supportive people who respect your need to heal at your own pace.

3. Mindfulness and Body-Centered Practices

- Techniques such as yoga, meditation, and mindfulness can help reconnect with your body, manage stress, and reduce the intensity of trauma-related emotions.

- **Practice Example:** Engage in daily mindfulness exercises, focusing on breathing and bodily sensations, to cultivate presence and reduce anxiety.

Developing Resilience Against Trauma

Building resilience is essential for moving beyond trauma. It involves fostering a sense of control, seeking meaning, and developing healthy coping strategies.

1. Empowerment Through Action

- Taking active steps to confront and overcome trauma can restore a sense of control and agency.

- **Empowerment Activities:** Engage in activities that make you feel strong and capable, whether it's learning a new skill or helping others in similar situations.

2. Seeking Meaning and Connection

- Finding a sense of purpose can be transformative for trauma survivors. It helps shift the narrative from victimhood to survivorship.

- **Meaning-Making Process:** Volunteer work, advocacy, or connecting with others who have had similar experiences can reinforce a sense of purpose and community.

3. Self-Care and Compassion

- Be gentle with yourself as you navigate your healing journey. Recognize that recovery takes time, and setbacks are part of the process.

- **Self-Care Plan:** Develop a self-care routine that includes activities that you enjoy and that relax you, like reading, walking, or spending time with loved ones.

Conclusion

Overcoming trauma is not about erasing the past but about managing its impact on your future. It involves understanding the trauma, employing strategies to heal, and building resilience. Each step forward, no matter how small, is a part of reclaiming your life and moving towards a future where you feel empowered and whole.

In the next chapter, we will explore managing loss and grief, further building on the foundation of healing and transformation laid out so far.

Notes

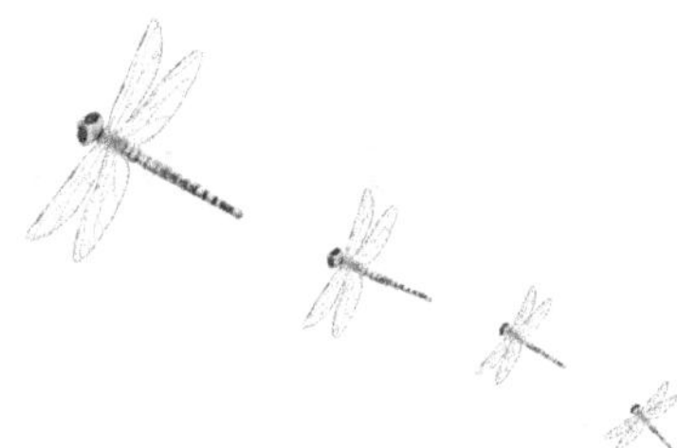

Chapter 7

Managing Loss and Grief

Navigating Through Life's Inevitable Losses

$\mathcal{L}$oss and grief are universal experiences that can deeply affect one's life and well-being. Learning to manage these feelings is essential for healing and moving forward. This chapter provides an understanding of the grieving process and offers practical advice for coping with loss and rebuilding your life.

Understanding Loss and Grief

Grief is a natural response to loss. It can be triggered by the death of a loved one, the end of a relationship, the loss of a job, or even the loss of one's sense of identity or future plans.

1. The Grieving Process

- **Grief often involves a series of emotional stages:** denial, anger, bargaining, depression, and acceptance. Not everyone will experience all stages, and they may not occur in order.

- **Reflective Exercise:** Recognize which stage of grief you might be in currently. Understanding your stage can help you cope with your emotions more effectively.

2. Types of Grief

- **Anticipatory Grief:** The grief that occurs before a loss, often associated with expecting the death of a loved one due to illness.

- **Complicated Grief:** Persistent grief that does not improve over time, leading to significant disruption in daily life.

Building Support Systems

Having a support system in place is crucial when dealing with loss. Emotional support can greatly aid the healing process.

1. Seek Support

- Reach out to friends, family, support groups, or professionals. Sharing your feelings can help lessen the burden of grief.

- **Support Group Engagement:** Joining a group where members share similar losses can provide comfort and understanding.

2. Expressing Grief

- Find safe and constructive ways to express your grief. Suppressing your emotions can delay the healing process.

- **Expressive Techniques:** Writing in a journal, creating art, or engaging in memorial activities can be therapeutic.

Coping Strategies

Coping with grief requires personal strategies that align with your life and experiences.

1. Routine and Structure

- Maintaining a routine can provide a sense of normalcy and stability during times of emotional turmoil.

- **Daily Structure:** Try to keep regular meal times, sleep schedules, and exercise routines to help manage stress and promote well-being.

2. Allow Yourself to Feel

- Allow yourself time to mourn and feel your emotions without judgment. This acceptance is crucial for healing.

- **Mindfulness Practice:** Practice mindfulness to be present with your emotions without becoming overwhelmed by them.

3. Plan for Triggers

- Anniversaries, holidays, and special events can reawaken grief. Planning ahead for how to cope with these days can make them more manageable.

- **Planning Tips:** Arrange to be with supportive friends or family, start a new tradition, or plan a quiet day for reflection.

Finding Meaning After Loss

Finding meaning in the wake of loss can transform grief into a more bearable experience and foster personal growth.

1. Create a Legacy

- Finding ways to honor the memory of what or who was lost can bring a sense of purpose and continuity.

- **Legacy Activities:** This might include volunteering, creating a scholarship in a loved one's name, or simply living in a way that honors their values.

2. Personal Growth

- Many find that their experiences with loss and grief lead to a new understanding of themselves and a deeper appreciation for life.

- **Growth Reflection:** Reflect on how the loss has changed you, what strengths you have discovered in yourself, and how your priorities in life may have shifted.

Conclusion

While grief can be overwhelming, navigating it effectively can lead to profound personal transformation and healing. By understanding the process, employing coping strategies, and finding meaning in the aftermath, you can begin to rebuild and embrace a renewed sense of life and purpose.

In the next chapter, we will explore reinventing yourself—a crucial step in creating a future after overcoming significant challenges and losses.

Notes

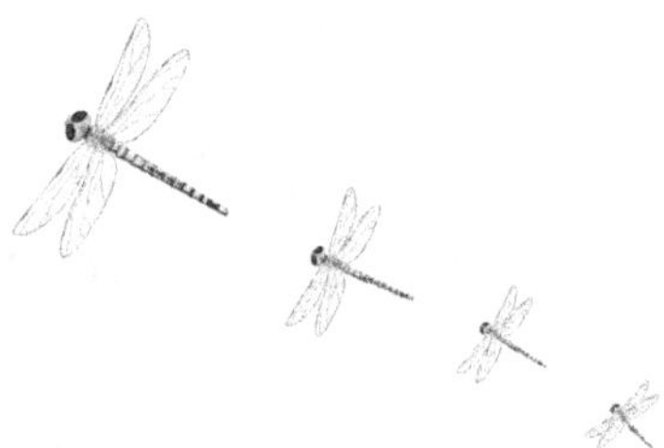

Chapter 8

Reinventing Yourself

Finding and Shaping the New You

Reinvention is about taking the raw materials of your life and experiences and reshaping them into a new self. It's not about discarding your past but about building upon it to create a future that reflects who you want to become. This chapter will guide you through the process of self-reinvention, helping you to redefine your identity and embrace new possibilities.

Understanding Reinvention

Reinvention involves a deliberate change in your identity, habits, and outlook. It is often sparked by significant life changes or a deep desire for personal growth.

1. Reasons for Reinvention

- Whether spurred by a change in personal circumstances, like recovering from a loss or overcoming trauma, or professional motivations, such as a career change, the reasons for seeking reinvention can vary widely.

- **Self-Reflection Exercise:** Identify why you feel a need to reinvent yourself. This understanding can guide your efforts and help maintain your motivation.

2. Components of Reinvention

- **Identity:** How you see yourself and how you wish to be seen by others.

- **Values:** What you consider important and want to prioritize in your life.

- **Behavior:** How you act and react in various situations.

Steps to Reinvent Yourself

Reinventing yourself is a journey that requires time, patience, and strategy. Here are key steps to guide you through this transformative process.

1. Define Your New Identity

- Visualize who you want to be. Consider aspects such as your ideal career, lifestyle, and relationships.

- **Vision Board:** Create a vision board with images and words that represent your goals and ideal future. This can serve as a daily reminder of your aspirations.

2. Set Goals that Align with Your New Self

- Break down your vision into actionable goals. Use the S.M.A.R.T goals framework discussed earlier to ensure your objectives are clear and reachable.

- **Goal Setting Exercise:** Write down at least three major goals that are crucial for your reinvention. Plan the first steps you can take towards each goal.

3. Develop New Skills and Habits

- Identify the skills and habits that will support your new identity. This might include learning new professional skills, adopting healthier lifestyle habits, or improving interpersonal skills.

- **Skill Development:** Choose one skill at a time to focus on. Set up a learning schedule and use resources such as online courses, books, or workshops.

4. Expand Your Social Circle

- Surround yourself with people who reflect the values and identity you aspire to. New relationships can provide support, inspiration, and networking opportunities.

- **Networking Strategy:** Attend events, join clubs, or participate in online communities that align with your new interests.

5. Embrace Setbacks as Learning Opportunities

- Setbacks are inevitable but can be valuable learning experiences. Each challenge is an opportunity to refine your approach and grow stronger.

- **Reflective Journaling:** Keep a journal to reflect on what you learn from each setback. This can help you adjust your strategies and maintain a positive outlook.

6. Celebrate Progress

- Recognize and celebrate each step you take toward becoming your new self. Acknowledging progress, no matter how small, can boost your confidence and motivation.

- **Celebration Ideas:** Share your successes with friends, reward yourself with a treat, or simply take a moment to reflect on your achievements.

Conclusion

Reinventing yourself is one of the most empowering journeys you can undertake. It allows you to actively shape your destiny and align your external life with your inner values and aspirations. By following these steps, you can navigate the complexities of change with confidence and emerge as a new, vibrant version of yourself, ready to face the future with excitement and resilience.

In the next chapter, we will focus on maintaining your new self and the changes you've implemented, ensuring that your transformation has a lasting impact.

Notes

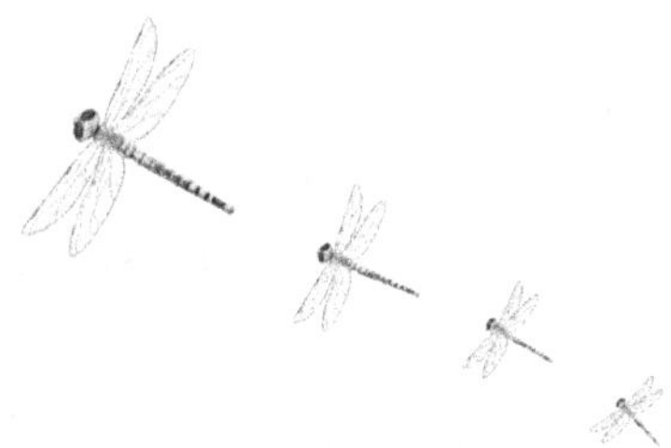

Chapter 9

Maintaining Your New Self

Ensuring Lasting Change

After the hard work of reinventing yourself, the next crucial step is maintaining the changes you've achieved. This chapter focuses on strategies to sustain your new self and prevent backsliding into old habits, ensuring that your transformation has a lasting impact.

Understanding Maintenance

Maintaining change is an ongoing process that requires continuous effort and adaptation. It involves reinforcing new behaviors and mindsets until they become integral parts of your life.

1. Challenges in Maintenance

- **Complacency:** After achieving initial goals, it's common to feel satisfied and reduce effort, which can lead to slipping back into old habits.

- **Environmental Triggers:** Familiar settings and social circles can trigger old behaviors, making maintenance challenging.

2. Importance of Consistency

- Consistency is key to making new behaviors and mindsets permanent. Regular practice integrates these changes into your daily life, reinforcing your new identity.

Strategies for Sustaining Change

Effective strategies can help you maintain your new self and continue growing. Here are some essential techniques to incorporate into your daily routine.

1. Continuous Goal Setting

- Keep setting new goals to advance further and avoid stagnation. Always have short-term and long-term goals to strive for.
- **Goal Renewal Exercise:** Every month, review and adjust your goals based on your progress and any new aspirations you develop.

2. Establish Routine Checks

- Regular self-assessment helps you stay on track with your changes and address any areas where you might be regressing.
- **Routine Check-In:** Schedule a weekly or monthly self-review to evaluate your adherence to your new habits and goals.

3. Seek Ongoing Support

- Continue to engage with supportive communities and individuals who encourage your new self. They can provide motivation and accountability.

- **Support Systems:** Maintain or seek new relationships with mentors, coaches, or peer groups that align with your transformed self.

4. Embrace Lifelong Learning

- Commit to continuous learning and self-improvement to reinforce your new identity and adapt to any life changes that might occur.

- **Learning Plan:** Identify new areas of knowledge or skills you want to acquire and set up a learning schedule.

5. Practice Mindfulness and Reflection

- Regular mindfulness and reflection can help you remain conscious of your new identity and the values you want to live by.

- **Daily Reflection:** Dedicate time each day to meditate or journal about your experiences and feelings as the new you.

6. Adapt to New Challenges

- Be prepared to adapt your strategies as new challenges arise. Flexibility is crucial to maintaining long-term changes.

- **Adaptation Strategy:** When facing a new challenge, reassess your tools and strategies, deciding whether they need tweaking to fit your current circumstances.

7. Celebrate Continued Success

- Regularly acknowledge and celebrate your successes to keep motivated and focused on your journey.

- **Success Celebrations:** Create rituals or traditions that celebrate milestones in maintaining your new self.

Conclusion

Maintaining your new self is a dynamic and ongoing process that requires dedication and vigilance. By employing these strategies, you can ensure that the changes you've worked so hard to achieve remain a permanent part of your life. As you continue to grow and adapt, remember that each day is an opportunity to reinforce and refine the incredible transformation you've undergone.

In the next chapter, "Living as a Dragonfly," we will explore how to fully embody your transformation, living life with a sense of renewal and continuous growth.

Notes

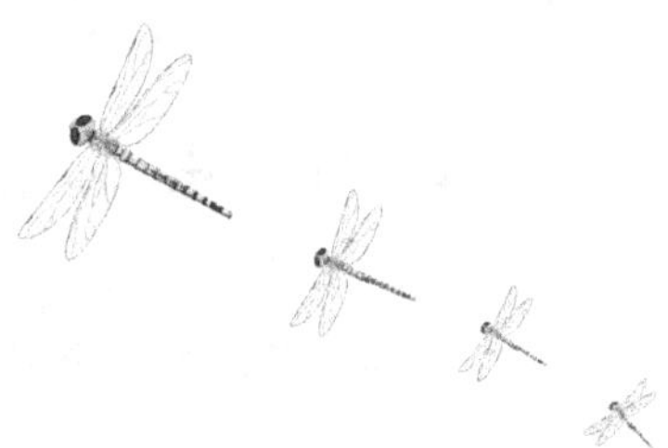

Chapter 10

Living as a Dragonfly

Embracing Continuous Growth and Renewal

The journey of transformation, like that of a dragonfly, does not end once a new form is achieved. Instead, it continues with living fully in that transformation, embracing continuous growth, and adapting to new environments and challenges. This final chapter focuses on how to live as a dragonfly, maintaining and nurturing the changes you have made while continuously evolving.

The Essence of Living as a Dragonfly

Living as a dragonfly means embodying the qualities of adaptability, resilience, and beauty in transformation. It involves an ongoing commitment to personal development and a willingness to embrace change as a constant.

1. Continuous Personal Development

- Stay committed to expanding your knowledge, refining your skills, and deepening your understanding of yourself and the world around you.

- **Lifelong Learning:** Engage in regular educational activities, whether formal classes, reading, or experiential learning, to keep your mind sharp and your skills relevant.

2. Adaptability in Daily Life

- Cultivate flexibility in your thoughts and actions. Adaptability allows you to respond effectively to changes and challenges, maintaining your stability and peace of mind.

- **Adaptability Exercises:** Practice saying "yes" to unexpected opportunities and challenges. Experiment with different responses to minor daily stresses to enhance your adaptive skills.

3. Resilience as a Way of Life

- Continue to strengthen your resilience by facing new challenges with courage and learning from every experience, whether positive or negative.

- **Resilience Building:** Set challenges for yourself that stretch your limits in various aspects of life, from physical fitness to intellectual debates.

Maintaining Your Transformation

Maintaining your transformation involves regular self-reflection, continued support from your community, and consistent application of the principles that have guided your journey.

1. Regular Self-Reflection

- Engage in daily or weekly reflection sessions to assess your growth, identify areas for improvement, and realign with your core values.

- **Reflection Routine:** Keep a journal or blog to document your thoughts, feelings, and the lessons you learn along the way.

2. Community Engagement

- Stay connected with a community that supports and reflects your values and goals. Community can provide motivation, inspiration, and accountability.

- **Community Activities:** Participate in community service, join clubs or groups aligned with your interests, and attend workshops and seminars that connect you with like-minded individuals.

3. Embodying Your Values

- Ensure that your everyday actions and decisions reflect the values and goals that are important to you. This integrity creates a harmonious life and inspires others.

- **Values Checklist:** Regularly review your activities and decisions to ensure they align with your stated values and goals.

Conclusion

Living as a dragonfly is about more than just enjoying the benefits of your transformation; it's about continuously striving for personal growth, embracing change, and contributing to the world around you. It is a commitment to living intentionally, with purpose and joy, no matter what life brings your way. As you close this book and continue your journey, remember that each day is a new opportunity to fly higher, see further, and shine brighter.

By embracing the qualities of the dragonfly—adaptability, resilience, and beauty in transformation—you ensure that your journey of personal change is vibrant and enduring, just like the dragonfly's flight across the water, constantly moving forward, exploring, and thriving.

Notes

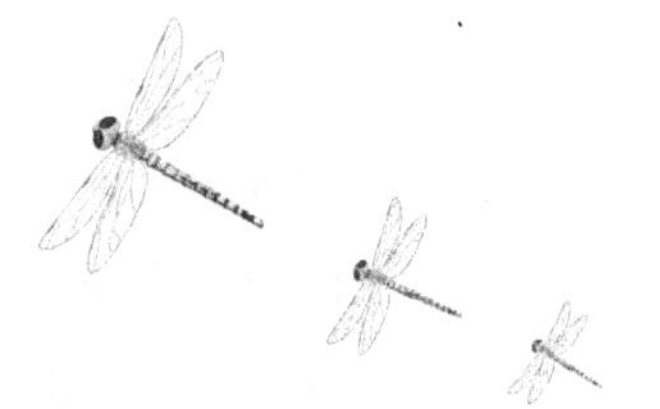

Final Summary of
"Dragonfly Where Change Takes Flight"

"Dragonfly Where Change Takes Flight" is a guide to profound personal transformation, inspired by the life cycle of the dragonfly, which symbolizes change, resilience, and self-realization. This book provides a structured, ten-step path to help you navigate through significant life challenges—such as loss, trauma, and the need for personal reinvention—toward achieving a fulfilling new beginning.

1. **Understanding Your Current State:** The journey begins with self-assessment and acceptance, recognizing and accepting your emotional and mental state as the groundwork for transformation.

2. **Embracing Change:** Readers learn to understand and embrace change, viewing uncertainty as an opportunity for growth and embracing the unknown with optimism.

3. **Setting Concrete Goals:** This step involves setting clear, achievable goals using the S.M.A.R.T framework, providing direction and focus for the journey ahead.

4. **Cultivating Resilience:** Developing resilience is crucial for enduring the inevitable challenges of life. This chapter equips readers with strategies to build emotional and mental strength.

5. **Practicing Forgiveness:** Forgiveness, both of oneself and others, is explored as a means to release bitterness and move forward, essential for emotional healing and peace.

6. **Overcoming Trauma:** Strategies for healing from trauma are discussed, including professional therapies and personal practices that help in reclaiming one's life and well-being.

7. **Managing Loss and Grief:** The book addresses coping with loss and the process of grief, offering practical advice for navigating these complex emotions and rebuilding life in their aftermath.

8. **Reinventing Yourself:** Readers are guided through the process of self-re-invention, learning to redefine their identity and embrace new roles and opportunities.

9. **Maintaining Your New Self:** This chapter focuses on sustaining the changes achieved, ensuring that the transformation is permanent through continuous goal setting and self-reflection.

10. **Living as a Dragonfly:** The final step involves living fully in one's trans-formation, continuously growing and adapting, and embracing life with a renewed sense of purpose and joy.

Throughout "Dragonfly Where Change Takes Flight," you were encouraged to undertake a journey of self-discovery and growth that is not only about overcoming adversity but also about flourishing in a new life created with intention and resil-ience. This will continue to serve as both a roadmap and companion for you as you seek to fundamentally transform your life, embodying the resilience and beauty of a dragonfly.

Notes

LIVING AS A DRAGONFLY